FIVE SIGNS

A Burning Light to Guide Free-Spirited Women, Witches and Empaths Through the Darkness

GW00585233

Alison Nappi

Author Website: www.writewithspiritllc.com

ISBN: 978-0-9975434-1-4

Printed in the USA

Published by Write with Spirit LLC

Dedicated to Nicholas (of the discontinuum) Harper and Hadith Harper, the gracious.

A special thanks to Tracy McEntee, who contributed to the creative process of Five Lies You Were Told About Grief:

Rest with peace and joy.

Contents

Welcome,
fellow travelers.

Moon dancers,
wolfish women,
wild god-men,
spiritual orphans,
fire eaters,
she-dragons,
daughters of Persphone,
ancient ones,
champions of light,
empaths,
neurodivergents,
witches and

survivors of impossible odds:

I knew I'd find you here,
between the pages of the world soul

reading the mountains and oceans and skies and
forests
like whole-body braille, with in-souled longing,
casting long shadows in dark places
wherein you are the only light.

With the courage of 10,000 armies and
the curiosity of an immortal you've
ventured into the darkness,
leaving your silver, shimmering footprints
in a place that is inverted

so the universal seed of aliveness
can bloom again.

Beyond the earth-shattering crack
of your own opening,
up from the rich, dark, blood-stained soil,
past the creatures of ominous worlds
and false lights and
into the majesty
of your own being.

I know how confusing descent can be.

You,
who find yourself in dark places
where you can feel yourself blink but
you can't tell if your eyes are open or closed:
Think of these essays as

flashes
of
lightning

to orient you
in your otherworldly surroundings.

Look for the Signs.
Let them show you where you are.

FIVE
SIGNS

You're on the
Hero's Journey

You won't feel ready for it, when it comes.

No one does. Castor doesn't train heroes anymore. No, your call will come when you are folding the laundry, punching the time clock, sitting at your desk with stacks of paper in neat and organized piles. One day, when you are writing checks, the wind will blow through you, and you will wonder where that chill came from as you notice your windows are so safely shut, and the room is a comfortable seventy-five degrees. This is your warning.

For those among us who are prone to leaping off bridges just to feel the thrill of falling, your call may not feel like a call at all. You might meet a tall, dark stranger who extends to you a harmless invitation and find yourself suddenly hurdling through space—gleefully—while cosmic dragons hurl fire that whizzes past your ear, singeing your hair, and giant spiders weave nets all around. Be careful out there.

Your call to adventure may come as a shriek in the stillness of the night while you lie awake ruminating about the rising waters, the secrets you keep, the way your lover turns away from you after sex. Or it might come as haunting and melodious pipe music you can only almost hear, being played by a nymph in the wild places of your dreamscape.

Your call might be a regal horn blown by the breath of a great angel through a million tree branches scraping against your window. Finally, if you're truly destined for greatness, your call may not arrive until the skies catch fire and set ablaze all the small comforts you've so meticulously collected, turning the house you were raised in to ash.

No matter how your call comes, it is the trumpet of your destiny. You will say that you have more important things to do: You are raising children, punching the clock, planning a vacation to escape from an oppressive life. You will protest to the messenger. You will say he has confused you with someone else, that you've not a heroic bone in your whole body, that your Honda, your atrium, your sensible beige walls are who you really are—what you see is what you get—and you simply cannot accept his invitation right now. You're too young. You're too old. You're not financially ready. You're not emotionally ready. You're blind. You're deaf.

It's already too late. When you are called, no refusal, no denial, no sputtering rejection can stop it from beginning, so don't go back to sleep.

01

The calling itself is your qualification.

You don't feel qualified? Good. Neither does anyone else. In the ass-backward and meaningless world created by our collective insanity, you must qualify. You must qualify to be permitted to work, to be housed, to have status as a human being. If you are batshit crazy and poor, you are diagnosed with a thought-crime from the big book of The Healthy State's Conformity Manual. If you're crazy—and you find a way to monetize it—you're eccentric and brilliant, a sharp and creative mind.

How strange, to give so much power away in a world that measures the value of a human life with numbers in a vast virtual databank. What is your life worth? Do the numbers add up? Are you qualified to receive the right to live with dignity and purpose? Do you qualify for healthcare? A safe home in which to raise your child? Food? This is a system that we collectively—and literally—just made up. It is insane. It is meaningless. Only our agreement allows it to exist at all.

Underneath all your concessions, your hold-outs, your hold-ins, your thrashing, your frozenness lies something original, unique and profoundly real, truly alive, bursting with creative ecstasy. If you have done everything right—even if you haven't—and you don't know why it feels hollow, how you've become so tame, so stiff and gray and boring, like the color has been squeezed out of you, then *your call has come right on time*. Pick up the phone. Fate knows you're home. Don't make her blow a tornado through your living room to get your attention.

02

Your life begins taking on magical or supernatural qualities.

Once you have been called it is not so far-fetched that you would begin to experience unusual phenomena. After all, you do not yet know what you are called to: What you will become could not be explained to you because it is not in your frame of reference. Can you imagine a color that does not exist?

Even as you take your very first step, you are blind. It seems unfair to be asked to walk a path that you cannot see, but in exchange for your lack of sight you shall be awarded vision. You will see with the eyes in your hands as you feel your way forward. You will peer into worlds that lay upon the dust under your physical feet; you will see the greater focus of existence, and you will learn to let go your attachment to appearances.

With any luck at all, it will start small: a glimmer out of the corner of your eye, a strange encounter with an old woman who says the oddest thing you'd ever heard, the sense that you are not alone in an empty room. You will wish to brush these off as tricks of your clever mind, but failure to heed the secret knowledge of your gut will only result in more powerful demonstrations, designed to dash the illusions under which you live to pieces. If you think the chill rolling down your spine in the silence is eerie, just dare to ignore it.

If you insist on physical demonstration it will come, but great risks you take with this demand, whose form you cannot control. Do you really think you are ready to kneel before an apparition as solid in your perception as your own body? Do you really believe that you could withstand the light of your own being without being shattered to your humanity? Would you become a prophet or an empty shell housed in the nearest nuthouse? You cannot answer these questions. You are too fragmented as yet to know what you are. We all are. If you do not think you are shattered, then you do not yet know even the most basic thing about your human condition. When finally you see yourself break, which may not become evident to you without great loss, only then have you begun to see what has happened to you in your sleep. This is the first hint to the true purpose of your journey.

03
You begin to lose your grip.

So tightly clenched have been your fists around what is left of your old life—of the pre-called self—that your fingertips have turned white, the joints in your knuckles ache, the ragged edges of your nails draw blood in half-moon shapes from the meaty bases of your palms.

Your old reality is now called into question. What was solid and true begins to warp and fade. The bedrock on which you built yourself is turning to dust beneath your feet. The walls on which you have hung photos of your dearest memories turn to ash before your eyes.

At every threshold you lose something: your shoe, your watch, your favorite negligé. Yesterday you needed these things; today the Universe teaches you that you don't. You're in a perpetual state of grief and wonder. In every mirror you will see yet another of your many faces. The days of being two-faced have ended as you discover, slowly, that you are everything that has ever been.

What a great and terrible responsibility that falls upon the awakening human. Ever more weary as you tread, you cannot return for you have lost your way in the vastness of yourself now.

Time, you find, moves in every direction. The alarm clock still rings, you still drink coffee, your body still sits in traffic, but your spirit is stretched across eternity. Everything looks the same, and yet, not at all.

Your skin becomes increasingly uncomfortable as you try to contain all that you are. You find you cannot stuff any more in, and so now you must begin to sort through the storage of your eternal self and cast out what no longer seems valuable, what no longer seems true, what no longer seems real.

You no longer look with your eyes, but with your inner sight. You see all the world, all it's devious systems, the way it lulls, the way it oppresses, the way it is designed against all truth. You have fallen for so many deceits. You can no longer trust anything you once knew. You begin to believe that this quest will claim your life, and one blink later...

04

The Abyss has taken hold.

Lost and empty, there is no longer a road, only darkness all around. It breathes, it hisses, and all lights go out. You no longer exist, and yet there is great pain.

All but catatonic, you lie there in your sweat, your tears, in the blood spilling from your broken and hopeless heart. You believe in nothing, in no one.

You are sure your end is upon you; you wish for it to come swiftly and terribly. You can do nothing but wait for your heart to stop beating, and out of this long dark night, a distant golden glimmer and harp music calls you through the boundaries of worlds.

Finally, you've broken. Finally, all of your defenses have been defeated. Finally, you have no choice but to see that all you have clung to is meaningless, that it could not save you. Finally, you have surrendered to the void.

You die.

You dream.

So many sights from a life now over: streamers and cupcakes, past due notices and pink slips, campfires and moonlight. Here, in the nothing you face your fears: no longer formless, they rise as phantoms in the dark.

War-weary, fightless, you watch them hang you and light you on fire, throw you from bridges, chop your head off on dusty cobblestone streets. You hear yourself screaming, through the long hallways of time. You hear yourself wailing from a cavern on the ocean floor. Your spirit has carried this pain since the first time you took form. You are sharing the womb with thousands of selves, frozen in the traumas of ages in human time.

You begin to realize what you have done. You begin to realize that your cleverness is not so clever after all. You start to see that your miscreations never die, not even when you do. You see that you have forgotten, but your creations never did; they cannot. They are bound to you, and you are bound by the laws you made for them.

You are ready now, to accept your undoing. You are ready to become a stem cell again. Formless. Helpless. You might become anything: a liver, a heart, a uterine lining. A star, a queen, a priestess. You've lost your will. You await instruction from the vast dark womb of the Mother.

05

You are ready to accept your transformation.

The cacophony of all worlds falls silent as you cross the bridge, the only direction you can now go. Behind you there is no life. It's funny how you glide now, swimming through the etheric soup, no longer hindered by your clumsy body, loaded down with heavy, dented armor or bags of worthless trinkets from a world that no longer exists for you.

It is dark in the womb, but it is peaceful. You have made it to the temple. You lost everything along the way, even your identity, which no longer hinges on what you do for money, or toxic bids for love, or what kind of car you drive. You are utterly empty and without will.

You have come to realize that you do not know what to be next; you've already gone to the edges of all that you know. Finally, you let yourself go into the arms of the Great Mother, whose embrace is a soft golden cocoon where your emaciated self can finish safely disintegrating.

The caterpillar cannot imagine what it is to be a butterfly. The sperm cannot imagine what it is to be a human. And ever so slowly, you are being rebuilt. You are being made new. You are going to be birthed one day, into a world you cannot yet fathom, into a life you did not know was possible. Where you have come from will seem like a dream, and your slate will be wiped clean by the hand of she who created you.

Though the home you now live in seems to get increasingly cramped and tight as you grow, you also have been given new ears and eyes, new limbs, a fresh and open heart, innocence.

You can sense the excitement as you float, you can feel that a new dawn is now close. You can hear their voices now, the voices of those who lit candles and sang songs and prayed for you to exist again. You can hear them speak of you as the welcome one whose arrival they eagerly await.

It takes some effort, the labor, it is uncomfortable, and your new muscles, new lungs, new eyes work hard to adjust as you squeeze through the same bridge you crossed as a tiny speck of pure potential all those long months ago, so you can emerge atoned, and blazing with soul.

You are no longer a slave, but a true and compassionate servant. Your needs are met just like a bird's needs are met: one day at a time, with the wind under your wings, and a whistling song that bubbles up in praise of the sun each morning. Your desires burst into being by the power of the divine will expressing itself as you now, unobstructed.

Your body, your brain, your singing heart exist only to embody Creation, as you, in a world that once seemed so scary, so dark, so dangerous. The dark armies are now like ant colonies. They climb over your big toe on their way to feed on the crumbs left behind by picnicking families, but they cannot see you, let alone harm you.

Now, the dark cities where you were chased by monsters are the playground of creativity, mercy, joy, peace and happiness. Miracles are ordinary occurrences, and you give them away freely to everyone you meet. Your breath raises crystal cities, and your heartbeat is the rhythm of the music that holds the universe together.

You are home again.

Then, the phone rings.

Pick it up.

FIVE

Declarations of Independence from the Norm

Don't believe them, when they tell you something's wrong with you.

The world is full of psychopaths, sociopaths, killers of revolutionary creativity. They're lying to you when they tell you you're a broken toy, so they can put you in a box with all the other broken toys, where you won't cause any trouble by asking questions, wearing hats or lighting the curtains on fire.

Insanity is a privilege when it's not aborted by the other, more common forms it takes in the world. If you see your madness through to its end, you will realize that true insanity has been rebranded as normalcy.

You will fall on your knees at the altar of your greater self as you come to realize what you really are. You will be appalled by the ordinary life. You will hear your own song for the first time since you left the spheres of heaven, and you will worship no truth but your own.

These people who have been given status because they've gotten with the program are not there to help you become free.

They will offer you a chemical straitjacket or some other kind of cage and promise to release you from your pain, but pain is just what you need to become your true self. It is an electrified fence, a vast virtual landscape that stands between you and all that is divine. It is designed to shock you awake. Don't let them take it from you.

Consider your depression, your bipolar disorder, your DID, your ADD, your PTSD as rites of passage. They may feel disorderly, but they are not without order. They may be perfect road maps designed to bring you through your shadow valley, and into the promised land. And you orchestrated it. Aren't you clever? Aren't you brilliant? And of course, they'll tell you it's not real. They'll tell you you're too sensitive, that your brain malfunctions, that you don't know the difference between reality and non-reality.

When you are tempted to believe them, look out at the ordinary world. Does it seem sane to you? Does it seem sane to you to live in a world where chemical companies are making your food, putting frog genes in your tomatoes?

Does it seem sane to you that when you look up at the sky, the sun is a faint, fuzzy globe struggling to be seen through layers of wispy silver clouds that emerge in long lines from military aircrafts?

Does it seem sane to you to that a faceless corporation dictates—directly or indirectly—when you can eat, sleep, smoke, shit as you sit for two hours in traffic, heat rising in waves from cracking pavement on your way to the factory line where you put screws into the backs of barcode scanners all day long?

Who would want to be sane in a world like this? Who would want to be satisfied, compliant, accepted here in the nuthouse of now?

Your inner pain is the chaos of the world. The war is inside you. The enslavement is etched into your cells. The silver skies are your pain blocking your never-dimmed, bright and shining soul from view. The distance between who you think you are, and who you really are, is a wasteland of lies.

Only you can create clear vision from blindness. Only you can pluck the diamonds from the singed earth. Only you can slash your way through a thousand miles of mazes: a techno-magical obstacle course filled with wizards and riddles, designed by you, and for you, to make your smallness feel real.

How else could you be a victim? How else could you show up for some meaningless drudgery for minimum wage? How else could you know despair? How can the sun see itself but through the humble eyes of earth? How is value understood without contrast?

If you're not traumatized by the ordinary life, you are already dead; you are a goat about to be sacrificed to the lion, surrendered on your back, waiting for him to take his fatal mouthful. What have you left to be scared of? What can you risk that is not already at stake? You've already laid down all you've come in with: your free and wild body, your mighty creativity, the solemn truth that seeks you in the deep night.

Here are some incantations to help you reclaim your brilliant and unique shine:

01
I am willing.

I am willing to stand on the precipice of the greatest adventure of my inner life and liberate all that I am from the lonely, dark, forgotten places within me. I am willing to risk all that I am for all that I might become. At least then, I will know. I am willing to leap madly into my destiny and meet myself where the worlds collide in celestial fields of glory and redemption.

Willingness is all that is necessary to begin. You don't need to pack anything else. You will become determined as you go, entranced by the infinite mystery of yourself. You will become invested as you find out what you're willing to fight for. Metaphorical blood will spill, resurrections will occur, immaculate conceptions will happen and points of no return will be passed.

You will become increasingly pregnant with the light of yourself and consumed with meeting the Christ-child in your belly. You are living the story that creates and dispels all myth, all religion, all the forces that bind heaven and hell to the sidewalks.

02

I am not the labels cast upon me.

They are like spells from small men with big hats waving sticks. I am greater than these. No spell within which I do not believe may hold power over me. I define who I am. I define what is right and what is wrong with me. I cannot be labeled. I transcend labels. There is no language that can hold me, no lie that can bind me.

The mind is shaped in large part by words. It is a meta-computer, referencing a lifetime of programming: tribal programming, cultural programming, national programming. It absorbs everything it sees and hears—on television, in church, at the flea market, in those little welcome packets you glance over when you take a job at the big box store, on the radio playing from a tinny speaker in the dressing room.

Your depression, your anxiety, your internal screaming is just a sign that the truth within you contradicts what you have been downloaded with, and the hospitals will tell you it's the blue screen of death. And they're right, it is. It's the death of the android self, the death of "Yes, Sir," the death of time cards.

03

The meaning of my experience is only that which I assign.

It is up to me whether I use my experiences to run toward or away from my true self. It is up to me whether my pain is a beautiful and ingenious means to sift for gold through many miles of riverbed, or just a cruel prank played by sadistic gods who get off watching me cut myself and complain.

If it benefits you to believe you're crazy, then by all means wear your tin foil hat to the grocery store. If you are comforted by having your creative responsibility stripped from you, then you have chosen to resign yourself to begging for crusts of bread and pennies from heaven while the vast riches of your true nature stay in a cave, guarded by a dragon that only you can slay.

As in every hero's journey, you will find the resources you need along the way, so don't worry if just yesterday you were a peasant sheering sheep. You'll remember where you left your dragon when the moment of truth is upon you. You will remember all kinds of magnificent things you've forgotten.

04

I am the expert of my experience, and the only authentic expression thereof.

There is no oracle with greater insight than me. No one knows this terrain better than me. I lead this expedition, and only the loyal, the courageous, the compassionate bearers of lanterns and secret soul scrolls may accompany me. Everyone else, step aside; you would not survive here.

Don't be afraid of the wreckage. Don't be scared of the dark. You are the dark, too, and in the beginning only the tiniest spark will light your way.

You will see almost nothing but the tips of your shoes, and you will straighten your ankle and sweep your foot out in front of you to be sure there is ground there, before you move: just one step. Sometimes, just a half step. And somewhere, in a world you can't yet perceive, your greater self will step toward you 10,000 times.

You will learn to become decisive as you come to realize what's at stake. You will find superpowers you didn't know you had. You will pick up rings of power and rubies and emeralds that you steal back from ogres and sorcerers and creatures your ancestors wrote myths about. You will use them later to pay back the gods of karma or to cross the River Styx with Charon. Stay long enough to be reborn.

You will bump into your selves again and again, and most of the time you won't recognize them: they will be great glowing angels, they will be raving red-eyed demons, they will be priests and will be star-dusted. You will fall out of time and space. You will tumble down rabbit holes inside of rabbit holes.

You will do impossible things. You will summon your weapons from air so thin no flesh could survive it. You will make things disappear, and reappear. You will scream, and topple cities. You will cry, and the mothers of mercy will come to you when you are on your knees begging. You will shape a new earth this way. You will write your plans here, so you can live them later.

05

The only way out is through, and I am predestined to win.

Even though it doesn't look that way, the game is fixed in my favor. The out-there is in here, and I am the Kali of this microcosmic universe. I destroy and create. I am creator and created. The resolution of opposites happens here, on these hallowed grounds within me.

We think that it's normal to be five-sensory. Things are simpler that way. In five-sensory reality, we participate in a shared illusion, and it comforts us. What we see makes us wretch, but when everyone is covered in vomit, it's en vogue.

When your spirit starts speaking to you, everything within you that is anything else feels it first, and in great chaos, it will rush at you and form a wall of fire through which you must pass.

You have been cryogenically frozen, and you are thawing already. The bondage of your encasement in ice is melting away, leaving you, perhaps for the first time, with a choice. To you, it may seem like many choices, but really there is only one. One glorious, blazing choice. One moment of unspeakable courage.

If you think there has to be more to it than labor and alcohol, then say yes. If you believe you are destined for something great, then say yes. If you know—and you don't know how you know—that somewhere inside you is something that has no master, then say yes.

Say a prayer. Write your will. Have an adventure. Bring an angel with you. Find God in the fire. Be changed, from soft and impressionable clay. Get reshaped on the way by the swords and the teeth and the claws of your inner enemies, and when you are perfect, you will emerge with a story to tell, and little left to fear. You will have discovered the wizard behind the curtain.

The world will still fear you because you will have found the eternal within yourself, and that which is eternal cannot be bullied, cannot be brutalized, cannot be stolen from and cannot be manipulated. This is not the state of the average or normal person, but by now, you've let go of normal in exchange for something of far greater value.

You will know it, and your very existence will be an impossible rebellion to suppress.

FIVE
SIGNS

Your Soul Mate is a Villain

He will come for you in your darkest hour.

That is when you are the most ripe, the most ready, the most willing to make a deal. You think your darkest moments are when you are crumpled on your knees, alone in the dark, trying to hide your sobs from the neighbors with the white noise of your TV. Darker still is the moment you rise, put on a fake smile and run out into the night, seeking to trade in the rancid stench of a decaying past for the pulsing, living, animal redness of the false-light night.

In but one moment of weakness you have betrayed yourself, and it is enough. This small self-betrayal— your slick shiny lipstick, your sultry eyeliner, your scuffless patent leather heels—lays the groundwork for him to plant his seed. You have forgotten love, and you wish him to reveal it to you, but this is not his purpose.

He will teach you about love by showing you that you never knew it, that you cannot tell a sinister enchantment from a divine light. This is his service: the mastery of seduction, of dark-lights, of torment and pleasure. You will fight him, but not for long. He is your date with destiny. He is an agent of all that tempts you to deny your truest calling. He is very good at his job.

There is no university, no education you can buy that will prepare you for this. Your professor's education did not come upon him easily, and his debt is not counted in dollars and cents. He has sacrificed and suffered and trained for this in just as many lifetimes as you have, and he is your fate-struck nemesis.

He did not need to look deep to see you heaving your heavy load, and like magic, he will light your grief on fire and drive it over the canyon's edge. Now that he has gained your trust, he knows you will soon belong to him. It is not difficult to capture she who does not occupy the space of her own spirit, and it is this pain that you have not yet identified that he will next promise to remove.

You do not understand the nature of your pain, but he does. Pain is his specialty. You think the hole inside you is created by lack, any lack at all, but really it is only your perception that is broken. You are convinced that there is something outside you that can fill this space, and you are secretly consumed by finding it. For him it matters not which false god you worship; he will conjure that which makes you weak. He will turn your eye away from the moon, and he will mesmerize you with fire and lightning.

Still not sure your leading man is a villain? Here are a few signs to look for as the path through the dark woods unfurls at your feet.

01

He gives it away too soon.

No sooner than you agree to take his hand, he offers you unearned rewards. You choose not to question this because you are in need, and he begins to tinker with your life in places where it is too tight for you to breathe. In your relief you will not notice that he is slowly wrapping soft silk ropes around your ankles and your knees. They are an extension of his touch, and you don't respond as you normally would to being bound, because you are beginning to hunger for the embrace of his power.

He will tell you that he holds you in his care, and you who have not learned how to care for yourself will feel safe. You have walked before with two-faced friends, but they were not nearly as dangerous as he is, because you knew what they were. But he is mysterious, and otherworldly. He is an aspect of your hidden self, a part of you that you have long-ago banished to the underworld, fearfully. It is his job to expose you. He leads you to frightening places, and shows you secrets you did not know about yourself. And you begin to change.

02
He extracts you from your former life.

You are running from something, and so you do not mind it when your doorstep fades into the background of your life with all of the comforting and familiar voices. In a dream you do not remember, you've already said goodbye. Deep in your spirit you already know you may never return from this place, and if you do, you will not be who you were before. They would not recognize you. They would not know you anymore.

You protest only weakly as he guides you past the boundaries of the ordinary world. A forbidden intrigue rises up from inside you, and he uses it to reassure you that you're safe in his big meaty hands. Just to seal the deal, he gives you an amulet he made just for you. You accept it like a chain around your throat, which, he claims, only proves he has taken responsibility for your well-being, and isn't that what you wanted? He has a way of making your shadow seem small, but you have not yet realized that it is only because his is so large.

There are many unusual creatures who reside along this dark path through the ancient hissing forest. Not all of them look fearsome; some are strange and beautiful, but there is an underlying disease in this place. You deny knowing this. You refuse to acknowledge that deep within you it is comfortable to be amongst the poisonous flowers, the meat-eating plants. The residents here know you by name, and yet you will continue to play innocent, and he will let you...for a little while.

He can protect you here, he says, because this is his homeland. And soon, this land will claim you too, because you have each forgotten the true source of your infinite selves, and have settled for the jungles of trickery and illusion. This realm has much to teach you, but it is a dangerous and seductive master who will not let you go easily once you've accepted its forbidden fruits. In fact, it intends never to release you, and before the long day of your life is through, you will go to war to save yourself.

03
He shifts his shape.

As you follow him deeper and deeper into the shadowy landscape you begin to notice things about him you have never seen before: the way his eyes change color, and his pupils change shape. The way his hands seem to get bigger and smaller, how his incisors sometimes seem a little too long for a human mouth.

He has delighted you with tricks from the beginning, but it is slowly seeming to you that a façade is crumbling with every step, and in moments when the guitar string is stretched too tautly you see him—for just a second—without his skin. You are startled and heart-sickened enough to pretend that what you saw is not real, and you carry on. You wanted to run, but it was as though you were bound, frozen, chained and guarded. How did this happen to you?

You love how he can twist himself into whatever you need: a silk scarf that slithers across your flesh reminding you of your femininity in moments when you are too afraid to be a woman, a bolt of lightning when the lights have gone out, fire when you are cold and hungry.

What talent he has, but you have not yet admitted to yourself the cost, as he is also changing your shape according to his needs. You are the bait when he must distract the two-headed beast to retrieve the emerald. You are the little girl he lords over when he borrows your strength. You are his concubine, accepting all his tastes as though they were your own.

04

He possesses you.

You are already too deep in the woods to find your way out alone, and you are counting on him to keep you from being swallowed by the sliding earth, devoured by what screeches across the treetops at night. You begin to see things out of the corners of your eyes: fast-moving shadowy creatures, long snake-like movements in the brush, eyes. In your dreams, he comes and takes you someplace you can't remember in the morning. He smiles, and tells you not to worry, that these are his pets, and you begin to see that you are too.

You have become loyal to him, as if your survival depended on it. You have been increasingly willing to accept that there will be times when you must beg if you wish to eat. You wish always to stay close, and when he ties you to a tree while he goes hunting, you feel lost and forlorn. You have begun to see yourself only in relationship to him; somehow, he has set up camp inside of you. Somehow, he slithers through your veins with your blood.

When you are without him, you still feel him, watching. When he is away, you still hear him in your mind. When you go seeking for something you need inside you, he is where it used to be, keeping the gate, rationing out your power and energy to you, on consignment.

05
He is (spiritually/emotionally/ physically) violent.

You didn't realize it at first: the way he was manipulating you. You were used to violence before you met him: you tormented yourself relentlessly. He alleviated you of the need to do this, slyly replacing your role as guard and tormentor, in a way that pleased you. First, he stripped you of your title. Next, he took your pain in his hand and told you it was now his. Then, he only used it to whip you when you hated yourself, and finally, he broke you at the hairline crack.

It is this shattered bone that is your salvation. It is this dark and sacred moment, when the hairline fracture inside you becomes a canyon, that you can finally see why your life was never working. You knew something was amiss from the time you were young, but never fresh—not innocent—

and you can finally see it.

You can't fail to see it now. It howls, and sucks a glowing, toxic wind from the singed and fallow ground you built upon. The castles must now crumble. The night must now fall. The dawn must now come. He, mistakenly, has unfrozen your time. The secrets you keep will now bubble up like boiling tar and you will burn to ashes so you can rise like the phoenix.

You are about to learn who you are for the first time in your life. You are already beginning to discover that nothing is as it seems: that the black hats and the white hats are indecipherable, when the grace is dark.

You do not know yet that the weakness you have shown is about to unearth Goliathian strength. You do not see that you are the giant, but you will, because your survival will reconfigure you completely and you will come to see that you cannot be swallowed, bought, sold or owned. You will find out that you, the maiden in distress, are really the great goddess experiencing a moment of smallness in a vast eternal fairy tale, where the beast shows you the beauty.

FIVE

Ways to Let Your
Record Stand

The art of writing is not for the fainthearted.

To write well—to write something worth a damn—you have to be able to see yourself as Creator. This may sound easy to the novice, but there is a prerequisite to this capacity, and it is not a thought, a mixed metaphor or a degree. It is an utter dismantling of everything you think you are.

We are all Frankenstein's monsters: every one of us.

Do you know who and what has put you together? Do you know whose eyes you see through? Whose hands caress your lover in the dark? In whose footsteps are you marching? To whose gut are you listening? From where the words you speak come?

You have been assembling yourself since the dawn of creation, and you have forgotten the origins of your parts. It is, in fact, probable that you have forgotten you have parts at all.

Are you ready for this? Are you ready to meet your demons, your ancestors, the mysterious ghosts that roam the hallways of you?

Are you prepared to do the math of ages, to root out the lies you live by and redeem them in print? Can you menstruate on paper? Would you tell your deepest secrets only to discover they are but a label on the lid of a box that has no bottom? As you write, you will resurrect everything from which you have been running. Can you look yourself in the eye?

Good. This is the beginning of greatness. This is the first step to becoming a writer. You are about to get the best education of your life, and you, dear friend, are the teacher. You are not just constructing a story; you are changing the world: your world, and really, what other world is there?

Your story is the story of all of us. As you reveal the stitching of your sewn-on fingertip, the welding of your elbow, the pins in your knee that make it bend, you free us all.

Are you crying? Put some fucking pigment in your tears so we can cry too. Everything about you—holy and unholy—is glorious, mysterious, unmapped and unconquered. What is more sacred, in a time in which even the elements have been bridled, than the wild terrain of your inner life? May your courage remind us all that we have not been defeated.

Your story is your gift to a world gone insane. What is true—no matter how relative—is a soothing balm to the spirits of all living things. Reveal your purpose to yourself, and let your record stand.

What the eff is stopping you? Your story is important and you owe it to yourself and the world to tell it. Hell, you owe it to whatever, or whoever, put you here on this tiny crowded planet. You owe it to the trees, to the rivers, to the children. You owe it to the ticking clock that counts you down to sleep.

Easier said than done, you say? Here are a few pointers to get your fires burning:

01
Ditch the shame.

Write your way through it. Where did it come from anyway? Under whose authority do you cower and hide from yourself and the world? Do you really believe that hiding what you are—which is what we all are—keeps the world in balance?

The old powers want you to hide. They are invested in your hiding, your cringing, your shame. They do not need to put iron shackles around your wrists and ankles. The shackles are inside you, and the slave-masters of the world are betting on your refusal to believe in something you cannot see with your eyes or touch with your fingertips.

No, you cannot touch it, but you can feel it. And you do. You feel it every day. Every time you smear a breast cancer–causing deodorant on so you do not smell human, you feel it. Every time you give it up when you don't want to, you feel it. Every time you put on sensible slacks and a turtleneck sweater and sit in traffic when you really want to wear fishnets and stilettos shaped like guns while you lounge at a bar in Maui, you feel it.

Stop feeling it, and write it.

02
Kick your inner critic's ass.

Whose voice is that, in you, that says "you mustn't," "you can't" and "you shouldn't"? Do you think that voice is yours? Do you think that voice protects you from chasing the red ball into oncoming traffic? Are you six? Are you really satisfied living in a playpen with the same toys you had since 1985, '65, '72?

They are hand-me-downs from your parents, and their parents. They are government cheese and GMO corn puffs in a plain white box with no decoder ring inside. Are you going to eat that shit? If you are, then you can't make art.

Write that dick a letter on pink paper and send his dumb ass to the unemployment line. You have work to do.

03
Stop making it all about you.

What makes you so freaking special? Do you think you are the only one who ever worked her way through college digging sharp spiked heels into a man's back for money? Do you think you are the only atheist who ever prayed for death after your lover left you over a text message? Are you the only mother who ever thought—even for a second—of hanging herself in a closet when you were so tired, so broke or so lonely, and your child wouldn't stop screaming over a blue phallic-shaped Kool-Aid pop?

Well, guess what? There are millions of other people who think they are the only ones too because no one has the guts to let it all hang out. They did not have the courage to show up for work—the real work: the art of being human, together.

But you do. I know it.

You are only the sculptor, the painter, the story-teller sitting by the fire. The material of your life—right down to your dimpled skin—is collective; you gathered it from the ground and it never belonged to you. You were chosen—for whatever reason—to get dirty and wet, to ruin your clothes and singe your hair near the kiln.

It's your art (life), but the materials you use to create it are borrowed, and it does not matter what your medium is. The profundity of your very existence is enough material to work with for an entire lifetime.

If you think your life is ordinary, then you don't know who you are. If you think there is no meaning in cutting the crusts off the bread, then you don't understand life. If you believe anything is random—anything at all— then you are squandering your opportunity. There is always meaning. There is always gold, but it is deep, deep in the belly of the world.

04
Call them out.

Are you going to let them get away with that shit? Are you going to hold it in your body until it becomes acid in your joints and deforms your pointing finger into a gnarled branch? Are you going to let the toxins of perpetrators' past float in your blood until your liver and kidneys give up trying and you turn yellow, or need a cold dead machine to keep you alive?

What are you doing to us? The world depends upon the visionaries, the schizos, the grateful broken, the multiples, the alchemical brilliance of lead into gold. Don't let them poison you. Bleed it out.

Call out that motherfucker who put a roofie in your drink, even if it was the school nurse, the shrink, your brother's best friend. Call out the parents who could not see you, who tried to fix you, who shaved off your beautiful jagged edges so you would fit into a box, "for your own good." Call out the bitchy snarling woman coming out of the salon in the Hamptons who visibly disapproved of your tutu and combat boots.

They were afraid of you. Every one of them. And with good reason. Unleash yourself. Use your wounds to heal us all. We are counting on you.

05

Embrace danger.

Dance with him. Snatch that red rose from his lapel—recklessly—and bleed. How else will you know what is inside you? You cannot avoid pain without avoiding the sweet scent of velvety rose petals on your skin.

You can dump it in a river, or hide it under a rock until it splits the ground beneath your feet and you fall forever. You can put it in a box and jump on it until it is compressed into a hard lump that appears behind an organ you never think about, but you cannot run forever. Eventually, you will have to choose, you will have to fight, and you will have to surrender to fate.

Why not do it now?

Why not wrap your legs around the neck of the beast and poke his eyes out with your tiny dagger?

Why not gaze deeply into the flame, and at the risk of burning your retinas, find out what makes fire burn? Why not sling yourself wildly into the seventh circle of your own private hell—screaming your war cry, sword in hand—instead of waiting for the dark armies to come and take you, bound and helpless, in the night? You are the kind of hero great men have written about for ages of human time.

And it's time.

Begin.

FIVE

Lies You Were Told About Grief

It isn't true that you have to get over it.

It isn't even true that you have to want to. No one else can understand what you have lost. No one else can bear the burden of your tribute to a love, to a life, to an identity now gone. What a privilege it is, to feel deeply.

Something happens when you entwine your fate with someone else. If they go somewhere you cannot follow, part of you goes with them. This unfathomable abandonment feels like birthing a baby who comes out of you: still and limp. You planned your whole life around this love, and it left you in a graveyard of relics you cover in white sheets.

You are helpless, as you watch the labor of your deepest love, your most sacred creation, disappear under the dirt without you. You want to hold it in your arms and join it in a sleep that never ends. You want to claw at the boundary of the earth between the two of you with your fingernails, but someone grabs you and pulls you away, and all you can do is wail.

You become hollow. You are missing a chunk of yourself, and no one can really see it once you put on your creamy lipstick and your designer dress, and you pluck your eyebrows and paint your fingernails and toenails to match. No. No one can see what you are missing; you look so well put together.

Maybe your closest friends think that you are lonely, but it is worse than that: You have lost the part of yourself that you loved most. The last period has been stamped onto the page, and yet somehow you were left behind, running your fingertips over a leather-bound cover slammed shut. You are a character in a story that is over, and since this never happens in the fairy tales you were fed in your most formative years, you are lost. You no longer fit in the world, and there is no star that can grant your truest wish.

And yet there is hope, but it is not the hope you want. Your sadness becomes all you have left and you begin to cherish it, to worship at its feet so you never forget the most important thing that ever happened to you. You hold it in your body and you feed it all your love, all your light, so that it stays, so that you can be closer to death. It will never sneak up on you again, because it never leaves your doorstep.

And they will tell you that you're expected at the office by nine. They will recommend that you still go to church. They will expect you still to celebrate at birthdays, and pretend it doesn't pain you when you must change your grocery list. No, you mustn't cry when you have to put back the soy milk because the only one who drinks it is gone.

Well-meaning friends and family will repeat the lies repeated to them in their hours of need, but they will not reveal the truth. They will not tell you how angry they were when this trite advice was handed down to them, how they took it with a joyless, tight-lipped smile, and an insincere "thank you," just as you will do. They know no other way. There were things they valued more than their grief: unsmudged eyeliner, making their friends feel comfortable, staying unemotional at work.

Their platitudes won't help you at all, but you'll hear them so often from so many directions that you will begin to wonder why you can't heed them. Instead of realizing the obvious truth—that the advice is terribly flawed—conditioning will tell you that it is you who are flawed, adding the burden of guilt to a heart already laden, gasping for air.

There are many lists of trite advice you can read about grief, and they will only add to your confusion about why you don't feel according to the grief map sanctioned by your culture. This map is supposed to tell you what is normal, but that map was not made for you. It was made to keep the engine of our cultural machine running. It requires your numbness. Refuse, my friend. Refuse with all your might to be numb.

I have no trite advice for you. I have nothing profound to say. I'm not going to tell you to get therapy or accept how life has changed. I offer you this in the spirit of "you-are-not-aloneness" and "there-is-no-schedule-dom." I give this freely from a place of "I-don't-know-how-you-feel-but-I-sure-as-shit-know-what-it's-like-to-be-devastatedism" and "This-is-how-I-feltity."

Can anybody hear me?

01

The Lie: You should be over it/him/her by now.

The Truth: No one has the authority to tell you how you should feel, when you should feel it or for how long. Do you hear me? There is no normal when it comes to grief. There is no quantifiable estimate of how much value who and what you have lost has added to your life or for how long you should be sad about that loss. You are not a machine. Numbers: days, weeks, months, years are meaningless.

Death and aliveness are inextricably linked. You may stop weeping (or not), but you will never forget the love, the adventure, the grandiosity of the effect that your beloved lost has made upon your life, and your character. In this way, death will guide you for the rest of your days.

Your life has changed forever. The touch of death is a part of you now, woven into the tapestry of your new and unfolding experience.

02

The Lie: You should stop talking about him or her.

The Truth: The only people who cannot bear to hear you speak of your beloved are those who cannot accept their own mortality. They are people who have never grieved. They either don't know loss, or they buried themselves with their loved ones. Trust me when I tell you, they have their own mountains yet to climb.

Those who would have you silence yourself, choke on the words that you must speak, are people who do not know their own souls.

I'm not a psychologist. I'm a writer, so you must know by now that I am having a love affair with words. I know how to make them sharp and pointy. I know how to make them sing like music. And most importantly, I know that they keep me connected to everything beautiful in this world, and the next.

Speaking of your loved one can keep their presence with you from far across the boundaries of the point where life meets death. It is a way to honor them, and a way to honor your feelings. It keeps their love alive in you. It extends the meaning of their life into the world in powerful and meaningful ways. It gives them back a voice in a world hell-bent on forgetting.

It's okay to speak of them, to them and even for them when there is good that can be done by you because they have lived. What better way to honor a life, than to extend this love to others?

03

The Lie: You have to move on with your life (right now). Stop living in the past.

The Truth: This advice is an act of violence against a grieving heart. It is a kick in the ribs while you lie hopelessly seized by despair. Whatever it is your loved one would want, it is unlikely that they would want an avalanche of guilt entombing you with your grief. You have enough to climb out of, enough rebuilding to do.

In many ways you are restarting your life from scratch, especially if your beloved lost was the central pin you'd built your life around. For many of us, there is no life to get on with; the lives we were living are irretrievable.

We must begin again, and we don't want to begin our new lives on a foundation of unacknowledged, disrespected grief.

Being with your grief may require you to sit amongst the rubble. You may have to watch a city crumble. You may have to let go of who you thought you were, in order to make meaning out of the meaningless tragedy of death. Someday you will rebuild this city, but it will be new, updated, your tastes will have changed, you will be more wholly yourself and your kingdom will reflect that.

04

The Lie: You could have prevented this tragedy.

The Truth: If your loved one passed in a sudden or unexpected way, somewhere inside you is a voice asking what you might have done differently that would have changed the course of events that led to the death of your beloved lost.

The truth is that the factors that influence the course of our lives are bigger and more mysterious than what we did and did not do. To hold yourself accountable for any reason is to deny the greater context in which life happens, and that is a dangerous choice to make, because it will eat a hole in your spirit that you can never fill without asking much bigger questions. Scarier questions.

How will I live with this loss? Will I survive this sadness? Will I ever love again? Who am I now? In what manner will I go on? How do I want to spend what's left of my life? How can I honor my loved one's life? And death? Is there more? What is the meaning of living? How can I find fulfillment now?

Why the fuck am I here?

05

The Lie: Time heals all wounds.

The Truth: The truth is there are losses you never get over. They break you to pieces and you can never go back to the original shape you once were, and so you will grieve your own death with that of your beloved lost.

Your grief is your love, turned inside-out. That is why it is so deep. That is why it is so consuming. When your sadness seems bottomless, it is because your love knows no bounds.

Grief teaches us about who we are, and any attempt to crush it, to bury it with the body is an act of vengeance against your own nature.

If everyone felt, honored, respected and trusted their true feelings, this world would be a different place. Instead of reacting, we would respond. Instead of judging, we would see ourselves in everyone. Instead of consuming, we would notice that we cannot fill the gaping wounds inside of us with trinkets.

Instead of pretending we are okay, we would take the time to wail, to weep, to scream, to wander the woods day after day holding hands with our sadness, loving it into remission so it doesn't turn cold inside of us, gripping us intermittently in the icy fingers of depression. That's not what grief is meant to do.

Grief has a way of showing you just how deep your aliveness goes. It's a dagger shoved down your throat, its handle bulging like an Adam's apple protruding from your neck, edges pressed against both lungs, creating a long, slow bleed in your chest that rolls down the edges of your life, and you get to handle that *any fucking way you want.*

If you have been sitting on old grief from your child-hood, your failed relationships, the loss of a family pet when you were nine and any other losses you were unable to honor in the past, this left-over grief will also come through the broken dam. Let it.

And herein lies the gift that cannot die. Grief changes the course of your life forever. If you allow yourself the chance to feel it for as long as you need to—even if it is for the rest of your life—you will be guided by it. You will become someone it would have been impossible for you to be, and in this way your loved one lives on, in you.

About the Author

Seek Me Out. Work with Alison

Alison Nappi is a wild creature made of dragon wing skin and fireflies and moonlight captured in the eye of the sorcerer who went too far. She is part wolf, part fragmented prayer carved in ancient tongues, part looking glass. Her actual spine is the place where pages come together to show you where you are. When she is not mapping the underworld, she may be found crafting spells for a new world that can't exist, or leaving honeycomb near the edge of a cliff near a river, or stomping prayers into the earth in wild heathen morse code 'round a fire on the edge of an ocean somewhere while men drum and women wail. You can find her, if you're looking through a hagstone, or by signing up for her Substack. Ask her for a poem to ward off the night, or to bring it in tighter, so you can wrap it 'round your body, and stay warm in deep space.

Alison Nappi offers coaching for highly creative, empathic, neurodivergent and spiritually-motivated writers, healers, and therapists who want to share their wisdom with the world. You can register for an online course or custom coaching program on her website, www.writewithspiritllc.com.

Printed in Great Britain
by Amazon